It Is If I Speak

WESLEYAN POETRY

It Is If I Speak

Joe Wenderoth

Wesleyan University Press

PUBLISHED BY UNIVERSITY PRESS OF NEW ENGLAND

HANOVER AND LONDON

Published by University Press of New England

Printed in the United States of America

5   4   3   2   1

CIP data appear at the end of the book

Romana,

sleep in front of me
until we are
distilled

OEDIPUS: Did you give him the child he asks about?

HERDSMAN: I did. I wish that I had died that day!

OEDIPUS: You'll come to that if you don't speak the truth.

HERDSMAN: It is if I speak that I will be destroyed.

CONTENTS

ACKNOWLEDGMENTS

Thanks to Heather for continually decisive guidance in the realm of sentences. To Stuart and Graham for secretly vital phone-calls and e-mails—and to Stuart especially for his suggestion regarding the title of this book.

It Is If I Speak

As Hour and Year Collapsed

We were a whole army underground;
we did not move.
We were replicas, at first,
but the army above,
that which we were shaped to resemble,
moved, spoke, faded, and came
to rot
in shallow graves above us.
We were never them;
even as the workers painted our eyes
the colors of their eyes,
even as they hauled us by torchlight
into the vast royal burial chambers
and made us to stand the way they stood,
once, above,
we were never them.
When our faces were finally finished
and our ranks were formed,
we stood guard over the absence
of the one who required us.
No one was allowed to look.
The chambers were sealed
and the last few torches burned down.
We stood suddenly alone in silent darkness.
We knew, though, that someone above
could imagine us,
and we could sleep standing up
in that image.
The workers, who painted our eyes
and carved our horses' manes,
could imagine us—the priests,
who looked into our faces and blessed us
before and for this dark, could imagine,

and knew that we were there.
But then they moved, faded, and came to rot.
We were still spoken of, as time passed,
but only as an *idea*, as though
we did not actually stand here
inside the earth, in these colors,
these unseeing eyes, this dark.
No one any longer imagined us as real;
we had to imagine ourselves—
the way we looked, the way we stood—
from the inside,
from the stillness of our own hearts.
And we did learn to see ourselves in this way:
blind, colorful, standing guard over nothing.
And we came to accept,
as *hour* and *year* collapsed
into one dull drizzle of dust,
that we would not be found—
our guard would never be relieved.
There are worse fates than this,
we told ourselves,
without speaking, without moving,
without anyone above us in this darkness
But we were wrong—what we told ourselves,
the way we stood, for years, in this darkness
was wrong—all wrong
And you, you bring how wrong to light—
you alone let the sharp light that forged us
fall hard on our faces again.
You alone remind us that what we have understood
has never been what we are.

First Impression

I don't like my teeth. I feel they are too small. They give the wrong impression. They mislead. And my nose—it conveys nothing of what I truly am. Come to think of it, my face, taken as a whole, is rather unattractive, and gives the onlooker a very wrong impression of my essence. I won't even go into my torso, or what there is beneath. It's as if someone had quite consciously designed these things in order to conceal me—as if, prior to my every appearance in the world, someone was able to get inside me and fit me with a subtle disguise. I have never fully understood these disguises, let alone been able to remove them. Each night I dream of shaving my head, removing my teeth, my eyes, my tongue, folding my legs up under me, placing my hands behind my back, and covering my skin with ash. It isn't so much that I want you to see me as horrific—as the final figure in a dream of this kind. No, I want you to see me as no different from yourself—I want you to see that I am, like you, mostly just the dream itself, that slow brutal vanity wherein the deft dissembling of disguises is as constant as it is unprecedented.

Promise

I will turn on nothing.
I will take my walk in the fire.
I will sing the song I hear
coming from the fire where I walk.
I will not look into the fire.
I will stay in my room,
singing a song I can barely remember.
I will turn into the fire.
I will sing a song I can barely remember.
I will bury my room in my bed
and carry my bed into the fire.
I will not hear the song at all.
There will be my voice,
just my voice,
and words that could never have been
in the song.

Meaning

I am gathered
too late
to
have been
just music

too early
to have been
the clean stone
from which it will not stop

coming

The Only Fortunate Thing

You have an idea of yourself.
It is a kind of building.

This building stands on the sound
of your heart-beat,
the imaginary width
of rhythm.

All night
it stands there.
On a sound,
an imaginary width.

It is fortunate, really—
really, the only fortunate thing—
that there is no one in the building.

Watching Home Movies

When night fell we set up the projector
in the grass by the snakepit, aiming
its rigid beam down at the writhing bottom,
and this is how we watched.
At first the projected light was solid—
no image broke it or held it back—
and we could see the screen for what it was,

a deep tangle of unmarried bodies
driven by circumstance to strive and glisten
in their failure to come apart.
We trusted in this failure,
and from within its glistening,
before we knew it, faces emerged,
as if to reward our trust,
and these we recognized,
these we could tease apart and speak of.
And we did, we spoke of them
until we spoke of nothing else,
and in the sound of spoken faces
and nothing else
we drifted into morning
without knowing
what we were actually looking at.

Native Quiet

this hospital is beautiful

yes   only
the wounded are thawing
too quickly
   too quietly
even as we speak

"We Sleep More Than We Sleep"

—Will Oldham

Strayed from productive disappointment,
now the unheard-of alone
will be sufficient.
Let its restless esteem be forever injuring.
Is it possible that your room,
in letting you be,
entertains this wish?

The Thinking Instructor

He does not signal the beginning of class. He sits at his desk and watches his students, who seem not to know that he is there. At a certain point, he understands that class has begun; at this point, he takes a very sharp knife out of his bag. He holds the knife up to the light and the students begin to see him out of the corners of their eyes. Holding the knife in his right hand, he holds out his left palm to the class. Then, carefully, as if drawing a very fine line, he pulls the blade across the open palm and lets the blood pour down. He cuts only deep enough to make the blood pour down. And he goes on like this, he continues, with deliberation, to cut, making parallel wounds. After he has made ten or so such wounds, cutting across the fingers as well as the palm, he switches the knife over into his bloody hand and shows—with the same gesture—his right palm to the class. This is not to say that the class sees—no, the class, much more than it sees the teacher, has resumed seeing whatever it is that is not this cutting. It is difficult to grasp the knife firmly, but he does so, and he proceeds to cut his right palm just as he has done his left. When he is finished he lays the knife down on the desk and presses his bleeding hands together, as if to heal himself. After a moment which seems alternately too brief and then too long to be spoken of, the teacher picks up the knife with his right hand, which has not healed, and again shows his left palm, also still bleeding, to the class. As he begins to cut again, in the same fashion, in the same wounds, the students begin to feel spiteful, and they try, more than they have ever tried before, to look away, but already they are secretly sensing that there is no way not to learn, and thereby destroy, the careful meaningless elegance that falsely distinguishes them from their teacher.

Orpheus In Hell

actual as teeth   or eye
holes   an always aching thing
bursts
     from his quiet shade
gathering up
          not his songs
but the intention of his songs
          —to begin the mutilation
which makes them memorable
     —to offend the gods
with the brilliance of the mid-air
that does not wait for them

Museum

The pattern is only ever of animal success,
the cry of a real gathering
misheard and losing itself
toward the idea of a sound
which was not a blade.

We are unique only insofar as we have learned to sleep
in this sound, or in the idea of this sound,
we are unique only insofar as we imagine
the pattern could be faded.
Our uniqueness, however, is all that really fades,
as certain cries cannot be tolerated, missing.

Send New Beasts

These beasts will not do.

1. Their bleeding is decidedly inadequate— from a distance they appear not to bleed at all. Considering the likelihood of distance in today's spectator, this is not a small problem.

2. While they are exotic enough in appearance—and I assume this is why they were selected—they have a tendency, and an ability, to hide themselves in plain view. I don't claim to understand this ability—I only know that it is widely felt that, even at close range, they are difficult to get a good look at, and this is especially true when a blow is being struck upon them. It's almost as if they're immune to isolation—as if they are able to always appear, no matter how alone they are, in the noise and confusion of a herd.

3. They are far too obedient and willing to receive blows. Indeed, they seem to sense when a blow is coming and to move intuitively into it. If this movement was desperate—graceful or graceless—it might generate some interest, but it seems to fall, tragically, somewhere in between. That is, they seem able, at every point in their torture, to collapse in a reasonable fashion, as if the collapse was being dictated by their own will. No one enjoys—I don't think I even need to tell you—a reasoned collapse. It is this aspect of the beasts that most deeply defeats us, our simple want of a show.

4. Their attacks—and I hesitate to even call them attacks— are largely indistinguishable from the active reasoning of their own collapse. It is as though they seek above all to expose us to this activity of theirs—to infect us with their will to reason, and in so doing, reduce us to the unvarying rhythm of their irreducible herd. I would like to say that we are immune to this reduction, but I am not sure. In any case, I see no good reason for continuing to subject ourselves to these attacks. It would be better to have no

beasts at all—to live altogether outside of shows—than to sink numbly into tolerance of a spectacle which fails to clarify what it is that distinguishes us from beasts.

Restrictions

No person shall be provided with genitalia unless:

1. said person is able to applaud believably

2. said person is appreciative of sunlight in at least most cases

3. said person is continually founded in a series of obvious nondescript colors

4. said person is in possession of an alternative to tonguing

5. said person is willing to apply forever

6. said person has demonstrated a negligible concern for the notion of industrial tenacity

7. said person believes, at bottom, in one thing

8. said person can resist the ugly selfishness of intentional celibacy

9. said person has some experience with creating and/or maintaining the snug

10. said person is pleased by the idea of having a "bottom" and is willing to debate and/or glare to preserve the idea

11. said person is made hungry by the foul echo, even as he or she understands it as predominately, and ultimately, inedible

12. said person is prone to at least one kind of destructive pouting

13. said person is fit, trim, and undecided

14. said person lacks genitalia

15. said person has "a lot" of personality

16. said person can guarantee that the provision of genitalia will disrupt, and subsequently disallow, the "success" of his or her career

17. said person is made antsy by the sale of safety-insuring devices

18. said person is able to sleep at least one hour (sixty consecutive minutes) per day

19. said person does not in any sense relish resembling his or her parents

20. said person is willing to see genitalia as a kind of modern extension of the alphabet

21. said person can gesture in the general direction of his or her doom

22. said person looks forward to seeing the genitalia of others

23. said person can remain calm in the onset of definitive permission

24. said person is capable of moving, humming, and thrusting as though determined

25. said person feels bound to be clean and to settle down amid clean others

26. said person can differentiate between male and female genitalia when it is important to do so

27. said person is not intimidated by the gentle sound of unmanned machinery poking the sleeping body of posterity for no reason

28. said person does not object to swelling, except when it interferes with speech or sleep

29. said person is able to remain awake for at least one hour (sixty consecutive minutes) per day

30. said person is able to stop what he or she is doing

31. said person is awed by the consistent discretion evident in the teeming heap of bygones

32. said person wants to live, if by "live" one means *resonate with difficulty*

33. said person is more hopeful when talking is not allowed

34. said person can describe his or her last meal

35. said person owns a vehicle made entirely of deceased family

36. said person is willing to swear allegiance to whatever is appropriate, even if this means abandoning his or her entire wardrobe

37. said person is capable of understanding climax as the simple disruption of property

38. said person is capable of demonstrating, without a word (as in charades), the very real difference between the womb and the farm

39. said person possesses a reasonably recent Baby Stain Removal Guide

40. said person agrees to forfeit the right to sue with regard to length, depth, or coloration

41. said person is able to appear humble on command

42. said person is able to stand his or her own aptitude in the realm of procreation

43. said person knows at least one person (excluding immediate family and sexual partners) by name, and is willing to report that person to the proper authorities (when it is possible to determine the proper authorities)

44. said person feels confident about determining the proper authorities

45. said person is not a freak, if we understand "freak" to mean any person under the sway of an Eidos that is insufficiently homogeneous

46. said person speaks in such a way as to conceal the several moistnesses to which he or she is loosely but momentously tethered

47. said person has penetrated his or her self by accident in the past

48. said person is vaguely fond of variety in what is perishable

49. said person is willing to submit his or her conception of animal hierarchy to constant violent doubt

50. said person is willing to insert a finger into an other

51. said person does not mind repetitive work

52. said person has always forded the various soft racks without being reduced to their seeming confluence

53. said person is not without critical holes

54. said person is of a mind to compose music for pornography

55. said person can enthusiastically deny having ever been anywhere

56. said person has penetrated his or her self on purpose in the past

57. said person loves to appear *available* in the deepest sense

58. said person feels bound to sing and bound to dwindle at the same time, which is to say, feels the future as just that part of the present that, in allowing itself to be carefully misunderstood, prolongs the fictitious flavor its real parasites will not survive on

59. said person stands in a certain way

60. said person is offended by the idea that the foundations were "reasoned"

61. said person has demonstrated an unusual grip on the usual, and is fond of reminiscing upon this demonstration

62. said person is able to keep the cause of laughter hidden from shame

63. said person is conspicuously without blame with regard to the specific course taken by that which resists extinction almost successfully

64. said person feels his or her head looks "just right"

65. said person believes the word "person" signifies, above all, a mobile, vacant, and consistently endangered habitat

66. said person is melting

67. said person needs a place to stay

68. said person is a qualified but uncertifiable damage-sound coordinator

69. said person is able to pray, in times of ease, for unrecognizable outcomes

70. said person has misplaced the bulk of what he or she has stolen

71. said person has elevated to gossip the incredibly subtle distinction that is there to be made between the two components of really fucking

72. said person perishes when at all accompanied

73. said person wears "outfits" and seems "together"

74. said person has excluded the possibility of significant motives when it comes to "life" and other such unthinkable entities

75. said person is willing to swear that he or she will adhere to all written restrictions, and to the spirit of partial, staggered freedom in general

Pretty Girl

We shall undercome.
The country we are dying for
dies before us.
These rooms are occupied
by forces we do not love
or understand.
Constant futile action makes sense.

Instructions On How To Get Here

Find a large, newly fallen leaf. Take a magic marker and print LEAF on it. Tape it up on the quietest door in where you live. Watch as it ceases to resemble itself. Watch as the word vanishes into thick air. Sweep up the dust when there's just a stem. Take the dust and dump it outside by the tree where you found it. Go back inside and pull the stem off the door. Now you are here.

Alternate Instructions On How To Get Here

Find a large, newly fallen leaf. Take a magic marker and print PIANO on it. Tape it up on the quietest door in where you live. Watch as it ceases to resemble itself. Watch as the word vanishes into thick air. Sweep up the dust when there's just a stem. Take the dust and dump it outside by the tree where you found it. Go back inside and pull the stem off the door. Now you are here.

All That Really Happens

My whole family has died.
There is a song about it.
I can't remember the sun on my skin.
Not remembering is a house.
There are no rooms in this house.
There are so many animals.
I would like to gather up one by one
the animals into my bed.
I would like to sleep with them
in the sleep that comes after the house.
My whole family has died.
There is a song about it.
The animals would sing the song.
Each animal thinks about singing
and then sleeps upon a tiny word-
colored plot of sun.
Each owes on its plot,
owes more than it could possibly pay.
This owing is all that really happens.

After The Mass Wedding

The music was awful
for awhile.
It came from wed bodies.

As the bodies came apart, though,
the music improved,
restoring in each one

the heap of pure luck
upon which something untrue
can be said.

This is what every
        body
was waiting for.

Lethe

Once, with my real father,
I walked on a frozen river.
We spoke,
I don't remember what for or about.
There seemed a bright cold day before us.
Something, it seemed, could not be forgotten.
We assumed it was the day.
But it was not the day—
soon the day was just words.
It was the cold.
It was the stilling of the waves.
It was how easily I could walk
to the other shore without him.

The Shouts Of Children At Dusk

the body of a man
        not quite sleeping
beside an opened window
            day draining as usual
in convulsions which resist
memory
                translation
massive infant hulks
secretly busy with their new dim
tit
    and in their wake
there is only
                the sick sweet stammer
he knows
would tear him to pieces
had it anything sharper
than the tongue of a child

Home

In a conservative state,
the idea is
revision is becoming obsolete.

Every state is a fantasia
of sorts.

Every minute your fantasia remains unrevised
is a minute devoted
to the inextricable ugliness
of finished room.

Not Touching: Thetic Perseverance

The we-machines don't work.

All the sleep's-blood-color
is wronged
into shape

by hand,
by missing natives.

Here we are.
Speaking of good endings.

King Of Illiterates

I have again spent the whole day destroying the archives
      kissing the wall of sun as if I was no one
  as if I was just this kiss
(decided from nearer than the nearest thing)
  as if I could have the dream picked from me
like shrapnel from a thigh
   —as if I could withstand the exhaustion
of this meticulous surgeon
insuring his conspicuous lack of descendants

drugged up
into the dying
room-shine
of this
obsolete hunger

an un-prefacing
I-sound
is netted
in a reason
for the coming
fast

you follow
this unimportant show

only so far
and without speakable interest

Wend

the place I sleep
is not
mending

components aside

I am
a wake
in sensing this

one-time

horrific blend

Obscenery

He says
when they made this place
they sure knew what they were doing.
He carries the dead woman
every day from her grave
in the shining sky down
into a small garden,
where a light snow is falling.
He is her lover, and he brings her here,
knowing he is not allowed to bring her here.
She sees the flowers he's planted
and thanks him,
and tells him what their names are.
He says he will never forget them.
They're lying on the ground
beside snow-dusted flowers.
She's in love with the ground
and the flowers,
but not with their names,
and not with him, who is saying them.
She hears him, feels his face
next to her face.
She wants to be in love.
Disappearing forever is the only solution.

Stalker

The bitten and shouldered and nosed
open nothing moving

sleeps carefully past your old weeping,
the dully wedged open dying

tent-light words make. It calls
for pulling up stakes, pulling up

light—it calls every hour for seeping up
into sleep's one word-beaten path.

Yes.
No.

There is no other way to remain,
it seems, in love with nothing moving.

Poem

emergency

to ogle

Palace Walls

I don't know when
        dying of automatic interest
I began to understand the sound of clones
as a great feast

I don't know
when I first spent a whole night
gathering up what has been said

as if there was something
            a sleep
inside

Inter Esse: Against Lap Dances

Our brief view
is best taken care of,
and most interesting,
when it refrains from insisting
that its brevity is a mistake.

To My Wife On Our First Anniversary

Strange to think there was a time
when the house was not on fire,
when we were not compelled to move
from room to room,
moving always closer to one another
and to the center, the final room.
Do not tremble to think of that room—
the smoke pulling the paper from the wall,
our eyes welling with meaningless tears.
That room, if it is a horror,
is a horror
only because it is a furious repetition
of the sudden adoration we have already
learned to be suspicious of.
But it is not the flame, it is not
the insistent arrhythmia of knowing
where there is no room,
that I am given to adore tonight.
It is you.
It is the way you let the flames come over you
when you sleep.
And I want you to understand me:
I need the flames to come closer.
How else could I see your face
and know that it is nothing
if not mine.

The Method

Take your eyes off of the room.
Do you see?
There is a luxury
from which
one does not recover.

Each Sentence Is Into The Fast

When none of this interests me I distort my jaw
so that my teeth touch one another in a new way.
The newness of the way is nothing
but the impossibly mild seizure of a stall
I cannot hope to understand or complete.
Nevertheless, I muster at the stall
until the newness of the way is old.
Until all that is new is the muster itself,
as though the devouring force could be turned—
once and for all—
into the fast
that even its simplest tools
cannot stop promising.

The Administration Of The Registration

It seems they're offering two choices. I can get kissed in the scenic area at the height of day, or I can get cut up into informative pieces while I sleep. I think I'd really prefer getting kissed in the scenic area at the height of day, half-asleep, *while* I get cut up into informative pieces. This seems like a lot to ask, I know. I'm happy, though, whatever way things go, so long as I'm not asked to live with the information that comes of me.

Unspeakably Early

The department of corrections mourns appearances.
In the evening someone brings fresh music,

and the store cleans itself
toward where we might show,

but it's never clean enough to end mourning
or to end appearances.

The long-planned dance ends unspeakably early,
and its executives drive home sad.

Only the slaves left to clean up the small mess
feel real good in the dusk,

leaning on its fatal impasse.
Such leans start families.

It could happen to any one of us.

Letter From A Most-Loved American General, 1996

I retreated with my whole army
into the countryside,
deep into the countryside.
This is the only sacred thing, retreat,
the only thing we have ever really believed in.
We moved deeper into the countryside
every chance we got.
If the weather allowed, we moved.
We came to a point, however,
where the countryside could get no deeper.
We knew, I think,
that we would come to this point.
We are at this point now.
And now, whenever we move,
we move *out of* the countryside,
we move *against* a city, *against* our enemy.
I have had to give the order *not to move*,
though this most certainly means we will starve.
My orders have brought no discord, however;
the men and I are one.
Even here, even starving,
entrenched in a dwindling countryside,
unable to retreat,
we remain completely devoted
to the one highest freedom:
the freedom to not have to speak of what we fight for.

To Julianna

Do not make a light that is not a fire.
When you have made a light that is not a fire,
do not turn it on.
When you have turned it on,
do not expect to see.
When you have seen,
know that what you have seen
is already only fire.

Things To Do Today

1. thaw the wounded

2. carry the portraits out into the sea and rest them upon the breaking wave

3. destroy the capital with picturesque caress

4. mention the inexplicably famous

5. dredge the lightest bunches (ASAP!)

6. burn the symbols as soon as bone starts to become apparent in them

7. decrease the drama to the point of gesture, phrase, a weathered and weathering yard

8. descend upon the living sound of propriety

9. gather the weight of *not having said* and place it upon the prettiest graves

10. organize and dispense an imperceptible *the*

11. perfect the ground

12. motion at the shore (as if familiar with the families there)

13. restore hunger analogies to the feast scene which has no before and no after

14. demand to see the sleep that has not been earned

15. motivate the habitually sick

16. sing the lack of anticipation upon which we are most certainly impaled

17. recall Mother

18. disconnect the vaguer images from one another and from the way in which we get on with it

19. determine the cause of the cause

20. facilitate the ways of children

21. earn what is needed for remaining beneath the sky

22. set the famous criminals free

23. force the unmonied nudes into view (and so, into wealth/ evaporation)

24. urge the animals to retract themselves, their lack of standard grammar

25. rouse the allegedly unpregnant from their unfathomable slumber

26. make the beautiful go to work

27. distract the keepers of the calendar and, when they are distracted, detach and destroy their unforgivable hobbies

28. people the pin-prick this evening alone makes in the atrophied muscle of common sense

29. grope and ogle the money machine

30. make a list of things to do in case of consenting adults

31. profit from the simple inability of a given body to own the breath it absently rides toward its own concept

32. get the fuck out (i.e. get to fuck)

33. develop humble obsessive donors

34. locate the words with which the deaf-mutes are never done thinking

35. mass-murder the animals with overly smooth minds

36. place a hand upon the brand new gash in each picture—not to stop the bleeding but to know it is true

37. prepare the eyes for the oncoming absence of voices

38. nibble at the warm stone of what has been

39. mourn the continuing success of the Snack Area

40. indict the misleading absence of spontaneity following each and every serious injury

41. understand nothing but the trap in which these many fine bones are inextricably lodged

42. produce a striking likeness of any one unproductive moment

43. be mindful of the ring-card-girl pose in oneself and in others, and be ready to make the difference a fateful myth

44. listen to the involuntary gatherers wishing for an impossible poverty

45. bless the bait shop employees who remain unopposed to an ongoing radical renovation of the idea of what is to be caught

46. collide with the hidden zoo and act surprised by the amount of unnecessary sleep hidden therein

47. picture the dirty dull scissors at work in the seeming seeming

48. refuse to pay the suggested amount

49. tremble with the hunger of cameras fixed upon a spot incapable of becoming predestined

50. oversleep

51. distribute faulty prevention devices

52. establish eligibility for the death penalty

53. clarify a morning posture

54. sing of eyes freezing, thighs giving birth, what have you

55. overestimate the degree to which the new scene, the scene that is just now being written, is fixed

56. overestimate the degree to which the new scene, the scene that is just now being written, is broken

57. lament those who are already on the way

58. postpone, for as long as possible, moving in to the sentence that is never not under construction

59. insist on the sad waste at the heart of all honest work

60. bury the elderly in the laughter that heals each instance of prayer

61. require the intellectuals to attend indoor night-time drug-taking picnics

62. complain about the way the various escalating dangers seem to conspire

63. nudge the drowsy lumberjack

64. adhere to the faint golden grunt (even when it dips into where it comes from, where it can't go)

65. use the definite article to make a broth

66. confine the untoward

67. polish the pre-birth emotion until it does not shine

68. mourn the health of the debonair

69. drudge the nowsy mumblejack

70. control the urge to farm

71. suck the body part of an other until there is a new feeling of closeness

72. offer help to the dying

73. embarrass that which abstracts itself from the secretly intentional clash of heads

74. endure the baby-sitting which knows no names

75. rehabilitate the truth tellers

76. devalue the circus tender

77. practice saying something

78. scrape the forgotten music from the great stadiums it accidentally built and failed to keep up

79. try to fluster the bulk of language with the idea of buried faces

80. discontinue the breadth of the applicable horizon

81. lance and drain the churches

82. define the deceased

83. derive the trajectory of absolution

84. attack the display

85. let yourself "go"

86. pray for the institution of a consistently glancing blow

87. mimic the open area

88. elaborate the impasse from which each orgasm seems to shrink

89. look for what's left of the portraits on the shore

90. post signs indicating relevant battlefields

91. expose the most casual technology in the world to the logic of its various fictional aftermaths

92. make the faithful look at us

93. weep new syllables

My Life

after Henri Michaux

Somehow it got into my room.
I found it, and it was, naturally, trapped.
It was nothing more than a frightened animal.
Since then I raised it up.
I kept it for myself, kept it in my room,
kept it for its own good.
I named the animal, My Life.
I found food for it and fed it with my bare hands.
I let it into my bed, let it breathe in my sleep.
And the animal, in my love, my constant care,
grew up to be strong, and capable of many clever tricks.
One day, quite recently,
I was running my hand over the animal's side
and I came to understand
that it could very easily kill me.
I realized, further, that it *would* kill me.
This is why it exists, why I raised it.
Since then I have not known what to do.
I stopped feeding it,
only to find that its growth
has nothing to do with food.
I stopped cleaning it
and found that it cleans itself.
I stopped singing it to sleep
and found that it falls asleep faster without my song.
I don't know what to do.
I no longer make My Life do tricks.
I leave the animal alone
and, for now, it leaves me alone, too.
I have nothing to say, nothing to do.

Between My Life and me,
a silence is coming.
Together, we will not get through this.

Human Moan

I am coming,
a part,

almost as if called

The Lie

our dreams are of a solitude
that cannot have been

we lie fractured together
in the way

we have spoken
each other's names

we kiss
the way

there is no light

Being

a song-bird sleeping
unthinkably slight   or bright
in a cage   in a dim room
in a night

not singing

the cage wrapped in bright paper
opaque paper
for thousands of years

and all that time
the dark shape of the bird
or the bird's soft violent flights

and all that time
a memory of the dark shape of the bird
or the bird's soft violent flights

and no sound
but soft violent flight

the cage wrapped in rubber steel plastic
the idea is to keep it safe

a memory of memories
of the dark shape
or the soft violent

that which we never knew
how to feed

no sound   no shape
it will never escape

what we have said

Knowledge

Morning swells until its shadows
are each other's
easy prey.

I know the laughing fast
with the carcass eyes of shadows.

It won't last.
The bit of noise
has never been swayed.

Nirvana

wings, the bones of wings
beaten upon the ground,
upon the sleeping fire,
unintentional,
the abdomen having been crushed to a tangle
of bleeding breath,
      erratic, lengthening,
and the sleeping fire shakes with the length,
and the muscles there still are
      keep raising up the wings—
a brand new fast—
and bringing them down,
the dumb span seizing
unintentional country,
      taking hold of the ground with wings,
knowing without breath
whatever sleeps,
whatever need be beaten

Juggernaut

I do get tired. Does it matter how? I suspect no. It's too late to turn back now. All I want is to forget you somehow. As if a face could prove untrue.

I don't get around too much. I don't have the patience. My beautiful wife lays down next to my dreaming body. I don't know what she thinks of it—she doesn't say. *Always*, what does that mean?

Insistence is nearness stuck on itself and adrift. I am tolerant to a fault. The idea is we are in the process of making something. Perhaps a narcotic. Let me see how numb you might be. Let me call upon the trench that has offered us, in some sense, to the discernible sounds of industry.

I am nervous. That's all. I transport through the streets a god that has been reduced to beautiful impotence. I wish there was someone who was not crushed beneath the dignity of my small progress.

Dream

a few obsolete machines
always
scraping and jerking

at where

nothing can be invented

Billy's Famous Lounge

I respect the dumb bastards.
Their faces floating in want
give me the strength
of the real current.
The current which would enter itself
as though it was not itself,
enter it from behind,
from under, standing up,
with a hand, face, tongue,
or the unspeakable soft root of names . . . .

We float this way, in want,
in the length of the loud pause.
Each chord of the electric guitar is a white petal
placed on real time, a moment,
already sinking.
The dumb bastards like the way
night's surface holds the petals up
and moves them—shows them up against the fact
of their endless disappearance.
They understand very well
it's all founded on a drain—
it carries us back and further down *in*
to where we just were,
where we're too bright to speak,
too dark to be spoken.
Where one wants only to go down,
and where one does go down.

I respect no one
more than the dumb bastards.

To Darryl, Who Is Expected To Die Today In A Beloit Hospital

Try to look at the pain
as the difficulty of making a photograph
of everything there is,
everything that cannot be saved.

Each sentence as it is spoken to you
is a thick column of light
falling
into your darkroom, ruining

that photograph, making you turn and see
the same old quiet shadows
huddled behind you.
They attend not the making of the image

you have come to need,
but the way you look,
the way you must keep turning
as it is ruined.

These are shadows, you want to say,
but to whom?
This is the sound of shadows.
The time has come to always be there.

"Existence Is Not An Adjective For Pain"

—Stuart Downs

the sudden impossibility
of summer's depth

     in summer

further evidences
its intention to oversleep
its best bodies;

you are a lull
not in sleep
     but in evidence

you are the most unbelievable of sleeps—
     the sleep summer cannot follow
or take back

Mishima

brake-driven carriage
lost in the steep
muscle of this drain—

have you a passenger still
who can bear
to fix the way?

Science

They tied the boy sun-
god
to a post in a field

and made a village nearby.

They wanted him to speak to them.

Some of them came each night
to make him speak to them.
This was why they were, they thought,
to be spoken to.
To make him speak,
they found they had to torture him.

This is why they were, they thought,
to torture him.
As they tortured him, inevitably
they began to take him apart.

Extracting a nail, a few lashes, a toe.
Removing an eye.

On these nights, as they tortured him,
he spoke, or sang (they couldn't be sure),
but he spoke, or sang, only to himself.
They listened to what he said,
or sang, to himself,
and took it back to the village,
where torture is unimaginable,

and where there is really nowhere
to put that kind of sound.
To keep it, they had to repeat it,
to try to speak, to sing, themselves.

Everyone in the village came to want
a part of the boy,
to bring them light, to bring them luck.
His body accumulated inside their homes
until there was a kind of glow—
brighter than the sky had ever glowed.

The boy sun-
god
got torn apart—
it was worse every night.
He grew unrecognizable to their children,
to their children's children.
The sounds rising from his mutilation,
his great pain,
were no longer understood as language,
or as song.
Soon they did not know
that this was the body of a god.
Soon they did not know
that this was the body of a boy,
that this was a body at all.
They came to think of him
as just that part of the field
that allowed them, increasingly,
to see inside their homes.

As they became accustomed to the glow
of the god's dead body (the inside of their homes),
they became blind to the shapes of the night
from which they came.

As they became blind to the shapes of the night
from which they came, they stopped repeating
what was spoken, or sung, there.

They came then to have no reason
to stand in the open field, in the night.
It had become apparent that the village
was now brighter, much brighter,
than even that part of the field
that could be harvested for light.
Soon there was a law against going out,
and just as soon they were law-abiding.

They live this way now,
in laws, in the bright loud rooms
a dead god affords.

Sometimes, though, they can hear their god
healing
in the night.
And they can almost remember,
then,
what it was like to torture him,
to hear the pain
lift his voice up
into something meaningless,
something almost a song,
something they might repeat,
and in repeating, begin to be free of.

Writer

A person, for you, is a book.
Impossible to categorize,
it veers from non-sense verse
to the most tedious of novels
and back
in just a breath.
And the book ends, the book ends.
And what makes the person more real,
then,
than a book,
is just that you cannot reread
one chapter, one sentence, one word.
You must rewrite him,
her,
and you cannot.
You cannot.
This inability is the source
of everything you have to say.

Go-Go Bar

      to sit there
into the moving lack of real
sources

the echo of uncovered works
dwindling

      to speak with and against
those dirty songs

(everything I know)

      this is our sentence

our cell

lit only by the occasional fist
upon the bone of an arm

Back River Neck Road

My first love
was the deep hiding sound
of the slave-path.
Slaves moving
the best parts of this light,
endlessly,
and never for themselves.
Slaves singing,
endlessly,
and only for themselves.
Slaves asleep in the way.
The sound of slaves asleep
in the way.
But then I myself was in the way.
And then I myself was asleep.
And now I move,
and now I sing,
but the slaves are gone,
the path is silent,
the best parts of this light
cannot be moved,
and I find that, although I know it very well,
I cannot make the sound.

"As Hour And Year Collapsed": The poem is spoken from the point of view of the famous terra-cotta soldiers unearthed in China a while back.

"Native Quiet": The line in italics is the entirety of a post-card I got from Stuart Downs.

"Send New Beasts": It was the practice, in Rome, in the old days, to slay beasts at the Coliseum. Not just any beasts would do, however—exotic beasts were needed. This meant that Roman politicians were constantly pressuring the governors of distant provinces to send them "new" beasts. Such epistles, I reckon, are more common now than they were then, even if they are less written down.

"Poem": Graham Foust wrote these words—my role was to make the decision to call them "Poem."

"Mishima": The Mishima referred to here is Yukio Mishima, the Japanese author.